GREEK BEASTS AND HEROES

The Silver Chariot

You can read the stories in the
Greek Beasts and Heroes series in any order.

If you'd like to read more about some of the
characters in this book, turn to pages 76-78
to find out which other books to try.

Atticus's journey continues on
from *The Dolphin's Message*.

To find out where he goes next,
read *The Fire Breather*.

Turn to page 79 for a complete
list of titles in the series.

Coats, Lucy.
The silver chariot /

2010. WITHDRAWN
33305225812357
gi   10/03/12

GREEK BEASTS AND HEROES

The Silver Chariot

LUCY COATS

Illustrated by Anthony Lewis

Orion
Children's Books

Text and illustrations first appeared in
Atticus the Storyteller's 100 Greek Myths
First published in Great Britain in 2002
by Orion Children's Books
This edition published in Great Britain in 2010
by Orion Children's Books
a division of the Orion Publishing Group Ltd
Orion House
5 Upper St Martin's Lane
London WC2H 9EA
An Hachette UK company

1 3 5 7 9 8 6 4 2

Text copyright © Lucy Coats 2002, 2010
Illustrations copyright © Anthony Lewis 2002

The rights of Lucy Coats and Anthony Lewis to be identified as the author
and illustrator of this work respectively have been asserted.

All rights reserved. No part of this publication may be reproduced,
stored in a retrieval system, or transmitted, in any form or by any means,
electronic, mechanical, photocopying, recording or otherwise,
without the prior permission of Orion Children's Books.

The Orion Publishing Group's policy is to use papers that are natural,
renewable and recyclable products and made from wood grown in sustainable
forests. The logging and manufacturing processes are expected to conform
to the environmental regulations of the country of origin.

A catalogue record for this book is available from the British Library

ISBN 978 1 4440 0069 6

Printed in China

www.orionbooks.co.uk
www.lucycoats.com

For Harry Cain, who loves my stories.
L. C.

For Bob and Rosemary
A. L.

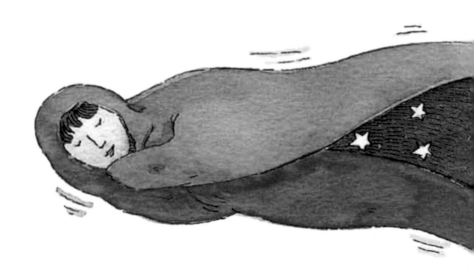

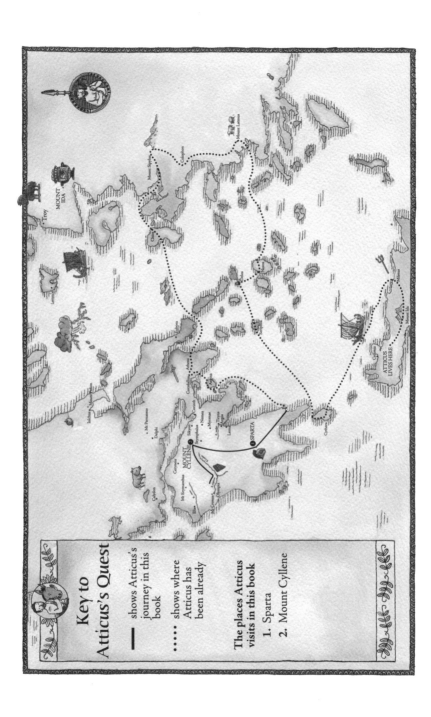

Contents

Stories from the Heavens

L ong ago, in ancient Greece, gods and goddesses, heroes and heroines lived together with fearful monsters and every kind of

fabulous beast that ever flew, or walked or swam. But little by little, as people began to build more villages and towns and cities, the gods and monsters disappeared into the secret places of the world and the heavens, so that they could have some peace.

Before they
disappeared, the gods
and goddesses gave
the gift of storytelling
to men and women, so that nobody
would ever forget them. They ordered
that there should be a great storytelling
festival once every seven years on the
slopes of Mount Ida, near Troy, and that
tellers of tales should come from all over
Greece and from lands near and far to

 take part. Every seven
years a beautiful painted
vase, filled to the brim
with gold, magically
appeared as a first prize, and the winner
was honoured for the rest of his life by all
the people of Greece.

Winter was turning into spring when Atticus and Melissa arrived in the great city of Sparta.

Although they had already travelled a long way from Crete, they weren't even halfway to Troy yet. They picked their way through the crowded, noisy market.

"Fine shoes and sandals!" bellowed the cobbler as they passed.

"Not as good as mine!" muttered Atticus. "Now, where's the barber's shop? I need a haircut. Nothing better than a barber's shop for news and gossip!"

The barber was busy sharpening blades when Atticus walked in. "New in town?" he asked.

"Yes," said Atticus. "I'm a storyteller and I wondered . . ."

"Hey!" yelled the barber. "This man's a storyteller. He'll tell us a story while I cut his hair!"

Atticus sat down in the barber's chair and cleared his throat.

Rainbow Eggs

The queen of Sparta hung her robe on a bush and dived into the stream. The water was icy cold, but Leda sang as she washed herself. Today something good was going to happen, she could just feel it.

At that very moment Zeus sailed by on a cloud and looked down. He saw Leda's perfect pearly arms raised above her head as she dived, and fell in love at once. Quickly he summoned Aphrodite. She was very sympathetic – love was her business, after all.

"If I turn into a hawk, and you turn into a swan, I can chase you into Leda's

 13

arms," she said. "I know she loves birds, and she won't be able to resist stroking your soft white feathers."

The swan flapped frantically up the stream towards Leda with the hawk swooping at its tail.

"Oh! You poor thing!" cried Leda. "I'll protect you. Shoo! Shoo! You horrible hawk!"

The hawk swerved away as Leda flapped her hands at it, and the swan nestled into her arms.

"What a beautiful creature you are," she said, smoothing its ruffled feathers and kissing the top of its elegant head. "Why, I'm quite in love with you already!"

Nine months later, Leda produced two beautiful eggs.

The first shone with bright rainbow colours, and out of it came the lovely Helen of Sparta, who later caused so much trouble to the Greeks and Trojans, and her sister Clytemnestra.

The second had a pattern of swirling silver mist, and out of it came the twin brothers Castor and Polydeuces, who became famous heroes. When they died, Zeus took them up to the heavens and made them into twin stars, where they still shine today, hand in hand.

Although she loved all her children very much, Leda was most surprised to have laid a pair of eggs, and she vowed never to have anything to do with birds again for the rest of her life.

As Atticus and Melissa walked northwards across the flat plain outside Sparta some men and boys thundered past, each carrying a spear.

"They must be part of the Spartan army," said Atticus, "Look at those horrible faces painted on their shields."

Just then a boy came running up. Tears streaked his grimy face, and he was gasping for breath.

The Silver Chariot

The clash of swords and the screams of fighting men rose up to Olympus from earth, and drifted in at the window of the palace of war. Ares, the god of war, was asleep, but as soon as he heard the commotion he leaped off his couch and shook his companion Eris, the spirit of strife.

Eris had a golden apple which was so beautiful that everyone wanted to own it. It caused a lot of arguments, which pleased Eris very much – the more arguments the better as far as she was concerned.

"Come on, Eris!" yelled Ares, strapping on his sword as he ran. "Into the battle chariot, quick!"

Eris grabbed her helmet and jammed it down over her spiky black hair. She had mean green eyes and a thin, sneering mouth which only smiled when her friends Pain, Hunger and Desperation played a nasty joke on some poor human.

Ares's battle chariot had just enough
room for two people. Its wheels were
armed with dangerous, pointed spikes,
and the black horses which
drew it wore silver armour
and had teeth as sharp
as daggers.

It swept down to earth and hovered above the battle. Ares and Eris yelled gleeful encouragement to both sides, and soon they were in the thick of the fighting themselves.

Suddenly a tall soldier with a yellow plume in his helmet came up behind Ares and stabbed him in the calf. All at once Ares began to cry.

"Oh! Oh! Oh! it hurts!" he sobbed.
"Someone get me a bandage! Oh! Oh!
Oh! I'm going to die!"

Now of course gods can't die,
because they are immortal
and live for ever.

Ares knew
this perfectly well.
But he always made
a terrible fuss when he
was wounded, because he was
a dreadful coward at heart.
Eris took Ares back to Olympus, where
Zeus gave him some magic ointment and
his wound healed immediately.

"Now go away and don't come back!" said Zeus crossly. He disliked Ares because he was so vain and boastful as well as being a coward.

That night Ares gave a feast for all his friends. He sat on his golden throne and boasted about how brave he had been that day, and they all cheered and applauded. But Eris just sat beside him and fingered her beautiful golden apple, and wondered whom it would be nice to upset next.

Atticus and Melissa had delivered the little boy safely to his army camp some weeks before.

Sparta was now far behind them to the south, and the hillsides were covered with a spring carpet of blue flowers. The stream rushing down Mount Cyllene looked cool and fresh, so Atticus and Melissa stopped to have a drink. A herd of white cows was coming down the mountain, followed by a dog and a young cowherd.

"Who are you?" asked the cowherd. "Nobody ever comes up here except me."

"I'm a storyteller," said Atticus, "and I'm looking for the cave where Hermes was born. Sit down and I'll tell you the tale."

The Baby and the Cows

Maia was the smallest of the Titans. She was always laughing and dancing and picking flowers, and all the gods were very fond of her. But the one who loved her most was Zeus. They married in secret, and because Maia lived in a deep, dark cave on faraway Mount Cyllene, jealous Hera never found out.

In due course Maia had a little son, whom she called Hermes. Like his mother, he loved to laugh, and a cheerier, chubbier, cuddlier baby could not have been found anywhere.

He was also very clever and loved to play tricks and jokes on his fellow gods. Almost as soon as he was born he sneaked out of his cradle and ran on his baby feet out of the cave and all the way to the Arcadian Meadows, where his brother Apollo's precious white cows were grazing on the soft green grass.

Apollo was lying quietly under a tree, singing a little song and dozing in the hot sun.

"Hee hee!" Hermes giggled. "Won't Apollo be surprised when his best cows disappear without leaving any tracks! He'll think a monster has eaten them!"

He tiptoed through the flowers and rounded up the fifty fattest cows. "Quiet!" he whispered as he bound up their hooves with birch bark, and tied straw brooms to their tails so that they would sweep away their own hoofprints. "Come with me!"

On the way home to Maia's cave Hermes felt a bit hungry, so he sat down and ate two whole cows. Then he took the long curvy horns and some other bits of the cows he had eaten, and made a lyre. It was the first lyre ever made in the

world, and Hermes was rather pleased
with it.

Soon he had hidden the cows in a
wood and sneaked back to his cradle,
where he snuggled down for a nap.

"You naughty baby!" whispered Maia
from her bed. "Where on earth have you
been?"

 29

But Hermes just burped contentedly. He had eaten rather a lot of cow, after all.

At dawn Apollo came raging and shouting into the cave. "Where are my cows?" he yelled. "I know you stole them!"

But Hermes just gurgled happily.

Apollo turned scarlet. "Don't you goo at me, you – you – **BABY!**"

And he scooped him up and whisked him straight up to Olympus, where he burst in on an important meeting of the gods.

"This – this – **INFANT** has stolen my lovely cows, and he won't tell me where they are!"

The gods looked startled for a moment, then they burst out laughing. They laughed until they were rolling about on the floor. Little baby Hermes looked so funny standing beside big tall Apollo.

"Oh dear!" said Zeus, wiping the tears from his eyes. "I suppose you'd better have them back. Show your brother where they are, you bad baby!"

And Hermes had to do what Zeus said. On the way he picked up his new lyre and showed it to his brother.

He ran his fat little fingers across the strings, and a shower of silvery notes pealed out and rang around the valleys.

 31

Now Apollo liked music even more than cows, and the lyre was the most wonderful instrument he had ever heard.

In the end Hermes got all the cows as well as Apollo's magic staff, just so Apollo could have the lyre all to himself.

And Zeus was so proud of his baby son that he made him the messenger of the gods, and gave him a pair of winged sandals, a magical winged hat and a cloak of invisibility, so that he could flit about the world unseen.

Hermes never stole again, but the gods and goddesses on Olympus always kept a careful eye out for the clever tricks and jokes he played on them every single day.

"Could you come to our Spring Festival?" said the cowherd. "It's only three days' walk, and the mayor would be delighted."

As soon as the mayor had met Atticus, he clapped his hands. "Silence for the great Cretan storyteller!" he shouted.

"Any requests?" asked Atticus.

A pretty woman stepped forward. "I'd like to hear a story about Corinth," she said. "That's where I'm from."

Atticus bowed. "Then I shall tell you the story of how Sisyphus of Corinth tricked the gods for a second time."

The King Who Tricked Death

Zeus was very cross with King Sisyphus Sharp-Eyes for getting him into trouble.

"Hades," he said to his gloomy brother. "I want you to drag that wretched king's soul down to your darkest pit, and leave it there for a very long time."

So Hades went off to Corinth to do as his brother had asked.

Sisyphus pretended to be delighted when Hades arrived. "How lovely to see you, dear Hades," said Sisyphus. "But why are you here? If you want to take my

 34

soul down to your kingdom of Tartarus,
you really should have sent Hermes
along. It is his job to take souls to the
Underworld after all."

Now Sisyphus was perfectly right, and
Hades knew it. While he was thinking
what to do, Sisyphus whipped a strong
chain around his chest and tied him to a
large pillar in the courtyard.

 35

There was the Lord of Tartarus and the Underworld trussed up like a chicken.

Hades was very angry, but there was nothing he could do. None of the mortals could die properly while he was tied up, and so the whole world ran around bumping into the souls which should have been taken down to the Underworld. It was all a dreadful muddle, but in the end the gods forced Sisyphus to untie Hades and let him go.

Hades didn't make the same mistake twice, and as soon as he was safely down in Tartarus, he sent Hermes to take Sisyphus's soul. But sneaky Sisyphus had dressed up as a beggar, and told his wife not to give him a funeral feast, nor to put a coin under his tongue when he died.

When he and Hermes arrived at
the river Styx, he couldn't pay the old
boatman to take him across.

"Sorry, Charon," he said. "No
money."

So Hermes had to take him round
the long beggar's way. Hades was even
angrier than before when they arrived.
The rules said that no king could come
into the Underworld without a magnificent
funeral feast and a golden coin under his
tongue. Sisyphus had neither.

"What a terrible wife you have," raged
Hades. "You must go back to Corinth
at once and teach her how to behave.
Really! What a dreadful example she
is setting to all the other kings' wives.
I shall have no gold coming down here
at all at this rate!"

So Sisyphus went happily back to

 38

Corinth, and kissed his wife as soon as he got there.

"Well done, dear," he said. "We tricked them nicely!"

Sisyphus died of old age after many happy years with his beloved wife. But Hades had his revenge in the end. When Sisyphus finally got down to Tartarus, he gave him a huge boulder.

"Push that up a hill," he snarled.

And so poor Sisyphus had to push. Every time he reached the top of the hill, the boulder rolled down, and he had to start all over again. He never did reach the top, and he may well be pushing that boulder still.

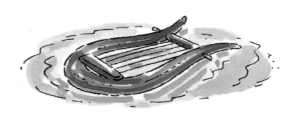

By the last day of the Spring Festival
Atticus and Melissa were both well fed
and rested. They had been staying with
the cowherd's mother, and his little twin
brother and sister, Phoebus and Phoebe.

"We shall have to move on tomorrow,
but tonight I'll tell them another story
about a cow, to say thank you," said Atticus,
as he filled Melissa's manger with hay.

The Hundred-Eyed Watchman

The goddess Hera was sure her husband Zeus was up to something. He had been acting strangely all week, and now she wanted to find out why.

Below on earth it was a beautiful calm sunny day, and as Hera peered suspiciously down from Olympus, she saw a funny thing. A black cloud was moving mysteriously fast along the ground, wriggling and shaking as if something was inside it.

Hera dived straight into the middle of the cloud to see if she could catch Zeus with yet another nymph. But when she landed, Zeus was standing there quite

41

innocently, stroking the head of a pretty
white cow with a golden halter round
her neck.

"My dove!" he said, smiling at Hera
nervously. "How nice of you to drop in!"

Hera smiled back, but it was a smile full
of danger. She knew perfectly well that the
cow had been a nymph seconds before.

She held out her hand. "Give her to
me at once," she commanded.

So Zeus gave her the cow. Hera took the cow – whose name was Io – straight to the secret garden which Gaia had given her as a wedding present, and tied her to a tree. Poor Io mooed miserably as Hera set Argus, the monster with a hundred never-sleeping eyes, to guard her. She didn't like being a cow at all!

Zeus didn't dare rescue Io himself, he asked his son Hermes to try.

"She keeps me awake at night with her mooing, and besides, it's not her fault that Hera's so jealous."

So off went Hermes, wearing a shepherd's tunic, and he skipped right up to Argus and tootled at him on his flute.

"Hello, old monster!" he said. "Still keeping a few eyes on things, I see."

 43

Argus grunted. He found being a watchman very dull. It wasn't like fighting other monsters at all. Argus was good at fighting monsters – in fact he had fought the dreadful Echidna, one of the two hideous creatures made long ago by Mother Earth, and killed her.

Hermes began to play a funny little tune on his flute. It was drowsy and dozy and sleepy, and very boring. Soon Argus's eyes began to close. First one, then ten, then fifty, then all hundred eyes snapped shut. Hermes tapped each eye with his magic staff, and Argus fell over dead.

Quickly Hermes untied Io, but as soon as she was free she ran home to her father, the river god Inachus. He recognised her at once, even though she was a cow, and rushed off in a fury to kill Zeus.

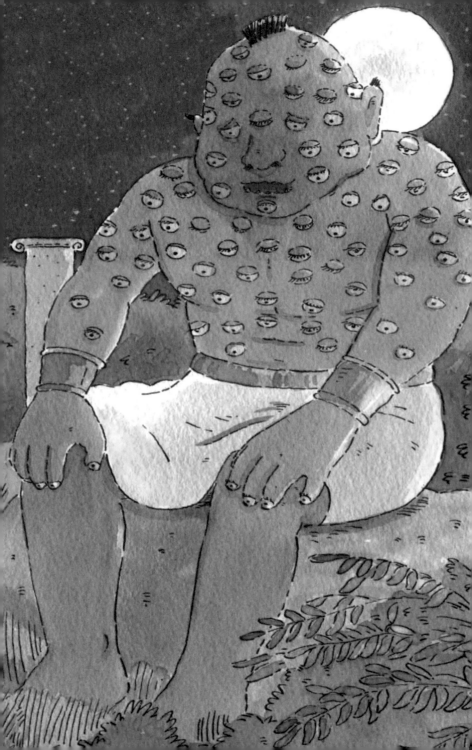

But Zeus saw him coming, and threw a thunderbolt at him.

When Hera discovered that Argus was dead, she wept and wailed. She took his hundred eyes, and stuck them to the tail of her favourite peacock, and there they sit to this day.

Then she sent a huge buzzing gadfly after Io. It chased her all over Greece, biting and stinging her till she ran all the way to Egypt. There Hera allowed Zeus to turn her back into a nymph, and the Egyptians worshipped her as a goddess.

But Hera made Zeus swear a solemn promise that he would never try to see Io again.

 47

Atticus wished he had never agreed
to take Phoebus and Phoebe to their
grandmother's village. They never
stopped chattering and asking questions
as they skipped up the narrow path
through the woods.

"How about a story?" said Atticus,
who wanted some quiet.

"Yes, please!" said Phoebus and Phoebe.

The Chattering Girl and the Beautiful Boy

The woods smelled green and fresh in the spring sunshine, but Hera didn't notice as she tapped her foot impatiently. Echo the nymph had been chattering and yattering for hours about one boring party after another, and now Hera had lost sight of Zeus. She was sure he was chasing some of Echo's friends, judging by the happy squeals coming from the other side of the lake.

"So he said to me . . ." Echo droned on, looking at Hera with a sly little smile.

Hera had had enough. "You're keeping me here deliberately, aren't you?" she said angrily. "Well, I'll soon put a stop to your chatter. From now on you'll only be able to repeat whatever anyone says to you. See how you like that!"

And although poor Echo tried and tried to speak, from then on she could say nothing for herself at all.

Now not far away lived a beautiful boy called Narcissus. Everyone was in love with his golden curls, his leaf-green eyes and his pearly white skin. But Narcissus loved nobody back.

 50

"Who could possibly be worthy of lovely lovely me?" he said to himself scornfully.

One day, when Echo was flitting sadly through the woods, she saw Narcissus sleeping in a patch of sunlight. She loved him at once, but how was she to tell him so?

Echo started to follow Narcissus everywhere, hoping that he would say loving words that she could repeat back to him. One day Narcissus was walking through the woods when he discovered a secret glade. The sun poured down through the trees on to a ring of bright green grass surrounding a sparkling silver pool.

As Echo slipped behind a bush to watch, Narcissus heard a rustle. "Is anybody here?" he called.

"Here!" replied Echo.

Narcissus looked round curiously.
Who could it be? "Come here!" he said.

"Come here!" repeated Echo.

Now Narcissus was interested. He
wanted to see this mysterious person.
"I want to meet you," he cried.

 52

Echo had never heard words she wanted to repeat more. She rushed out of the bushes, her arms held wide, ready to throw them around her beloved. But the loss of her voice had made Echo fade away until she was withered and wrinkled and so thin that she was almost transparent.

 53

"Go away! Don't touch me!" cried Narcissus and he ran towards the beautiful pool.

"Touch me!" wailed Echo sadly.

As she watched, Narcissus seemed to see something in the pool. He reached out to the water, but as he did so, the pool broke up into a million shining ripples.

"Oh!" he cried. "I have found the only one worthy of lovely, lovely me at last! But where is he? Where has he gone?"

Scornful Narcissus had finally been caught – but he had fallen in love with his own reflection.

For days and days he sat by the pool, trying and trying to reach the boy who lived under the silver water while Echo looked on.

"Alas, I cannot have you!" he sobbed,

 54

and Echo flitted mournfully round the
pool as she repeated his words after him.

Soon Narcissus began to fade away
too. His golden hair shrank into a small
circle of orange, and his pearly skin
surrounded it with white petals.

Finally, nothing but a small, white
flower lay on the ground beside the pool.

Echo kissed the flower as it faded and
died, then she herself became nothing
but a wisp of voice hovering in the woods
and rocks.

And if you shout loudly enough in
the right place, Echo will hear you and
yes, she will reply. *Yes, she will reply.*

"Peace at last!" said Atticus to Melissa a week later after they had dropped the twins off with their grandmother. "I've never met a noisier pair of six-year-olds!"

As the moon rose over the woods of Arcadia, they settled down for the night by a pool.

Just then, a great stag walked out of the trees. His coat was silver in the moonlight. As he put his head down to drink, a single hound bayed in the distance. In an instant the stag had gone.

"It's like the story of Artemis and Actaeon," whispered Atticus.

The Huntress in the Pool

Artemis the huntress stood polishing her great silver bow, while Zeus looked on proudly.

"What was it you wanted me for, dear daughter?" he asked.

"Just a little thing, father," said Artemis. "I love my life in the woods and I love to be free, so please, dear, dear Zeus, don't ever make me marry anyone."

Zeus was rather startled, but he wanted to please his daughter so he agreed.

"I shall give you a golden chariot, fifty nymphs to guard you, and a pack of my best hounds, so you may run free through the woods for ever."

 57

"Thank you," said Artemis, kissing him on the forehead.

Artemis had a lovely time hunting the deer and the wild boar with her nymphs and her lollopy, loppy-eared lemon-spotted hounds.

At first the nymphs pulled her chariot themselves, but then Artemis captured four of the five magical hinds who lived on the slopes of Mount Ceryneia, and she trained them to pull the chariot instead. Sometimes Artemis was joined by her

best friend Orion, but most of the time she hunted alone.

One evening, when the moon was hanging heavy and golden in the sky, a brave young hunter called Actaeon set out with his pack of hounds to chase a great white stag which he had heard was loose in the forest.

Soon the hounds were belling and baying and barking through the woods, with Actaeon hard on their heels. All at once he crashed into a clearing.

The moonlight shone on the pool in the middle where a beautiful maiden was bathing. A pack of lemon-yellow spotted hounds sat on the bank behind her, growling.

Actaeon stood and stared with his mouth open in amazement.

"Wretched hunter!" shouted the maiden. "How dare you interrupt my

bath. No man may see the goddess Artemis bare!"

And she scooped up some water and flung it at Actaeon's head.

As soon as the drops started to run down his cheeks, Actaeon felt something strange happening to him. His body thickened and became covered in coarse white hair, his arms and legs lengthened and grew hooves, and his head sprouted a pair of magnificent antlers.

Actaeon the stag lifted his head and roared with anguish, as his own hounds leaped on him and tore him to pieces.

"He did make a beautiful stag, but he shouldn't have looked," said Artemis, climbing out to dry herself, as she patted his hounds gently.

Afterwards she took them into her own pack, and when they died, she sent them to hunt with Orion among the stars.

Atticus and Melissa plodded on under the rustling leaves, until they came to a bend where two large rivers met. A flock of sheep baaed and jangled their bells as they drank. In the distance sat a shepherd boy playing a set of reed pipes.

"My feet are sore, Melissa, and we've walked a long way since we left home," said Atticus. "I shall dangle my toes in the river and tell you the story of Pan and Syrinx."

The Reed Nymph

In the wooded mountains of Arcady, where the nights are chilly, and the sunlight falls thin and cool through the still green leaves, there lived a beautiful nymph called Syrinx.

Every morning she jumped out of her bed of soft moss, and put on her dress of

mist and silken spiderwebs.

Then she picked up her horn bow, and ran through the woods with her sisters, chasing the deer, and leaping over the earth as light as thistledown, and as soft as feathers.

Every evening she and her sisters sang and danced with the friendly fauns or swam with the merry river spirits, and later they all feasted on dewdrops and honey nectar by the banks of the river Ladon.

Sometimes, when there were festivals and races on Mount Cronus, she would go and visit her cousins, who were the handmaidens of the goddess Artemis.

Since Syrinx was so beautiful, many satyrs and spirits were in love with her, but she always laughed at them and ran away.

"Can't catch me!" she called over one slim shoulder, leaping and darting between the trees. And it was true, none of them ever could.

But one day, as she was coming back from Mount Cronus, singing a sweet song to herself, the god Pan passed by. He had great hairy goat legs and a stubby goat

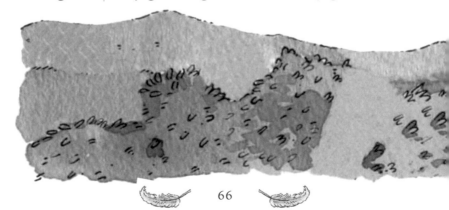

tail, and short twisted horns sticking out of the curly hair on his head. He was very ugly, with a wrinkled face, and a chin that stuck out. When he heard Syrinx's voice, he fell in love with her at once.

He straightened the scruffy wreath of pine cones on his head, and lolloped towards her.

"O beautiful nymph," he shouted in his harsh, rasping voice. "Come and marry me! I will give you fire-gold and emeralds from the forge of Hephaestus. I will clothe you in the silk of the sunrise, and make you a lyre of phoenix feathers if only you will come away with me and sing me to sleep every night!"

Syrinx looked at him and giggled. He really was very hideous. And besides, she didn't want to marry a goaty old god. She wanted to be free to sing and run and play with her sisters in the woods.

So she stuck her tongue out and wiggled her bottom at him rudely. "Silly old Pan!" she cried. "Who'd marry you?" And then she ran away.

Now everyone knows it doesn't do to be rude to a god. And silly Syrinx had just been very rude indeed. So Pan lost his temper.

"Wretched nymph!" he roared. "Just you wait! I shall catch you and keep you chained up for ever and ever if you don't do as I ask!"

Pan began to run after Syrinx on his strong goaty legs, and soon he began to gain. Syrinx dodged and darted between tree trunks, and over rocks, and under branches, but it was no good. She could hear Pan's hot breath panting as he came closer and closer.

She began to be very afraid, and as she approached the river Ladon, she cried out to her friends the river-spirits to save her.

Pan caught up with the terrified Syrinx as she fell gasping at the water's edge, but as he reached out to grasp her arm, the river spirits transformed her, and Pan was left holding nothing but a bundle of marsh reeds in his hand.

As Pan looked down at all that was left of the beautiful nymph, a little puff of wind blew through the reeds in his fingers and set them singing.

Pan was enchanted by the sweetness of the music. He cut the reeds into unequal lengths, and bound them together with wax and gossamer.

"Now we shall really be together for always, lovely Syrinx," he said. "I shall carry you next to my heart for ever, and you shall talk to me, and sing to me when I am sad!"

Pan taught his friends the shepherds to make pipes just like his, and to play them to their sheep, so that the beautiful voice of Syrinx the nymph should never be forgotten in the land of Greece.

"Who's there?" called a cracked old voice
at the door of a cottage.

"My name is Atticus the Storyteller.
My donkey and I need a bite to eat and
a bit of straw to lie on for the night in
exchange for a tale or two."

The door opened and a very old lady
hobbled out. "Come in, dearie," she said.
"I like company."

Then she looked down at her wrinkled
hands. "I'm getting near my life's end, you
know? So tell me the story of the spinner
and the weaver and the cutter of threads.
I'm a weaver myself."

The Cloth of Life

In the time before time, Nyx the goddess of Night spread her great cloak around the universe and held it close.

"Hush!" she sang. "Sleep!" And the universe slept.

Deep inside Nyx grew three stars, and the stars became powerful and strong. Soon they were stronger than their mother, and they commanded that she should unwrap the universe and share it with Day. Nyx agreed. But as she unwrapped her cloak, the three stars fell to earth and changed into three tall women.

The first was a young maiden.

"I shall spin the threads of life," she

 72

sang as she twirled her spindle. "I shall spin the red thread of anger and the blue thread of calm, the white thread of peace and joy and the black thread of despair."

And she set to work at once.

The second was a beautiful woman.

"I shall decide the length of the threads of life," she sang as she took out a measuring tape. "I shall measure up heroes who live short lives and cowards who live long. I shall decide when death will come knocking on

 73

the doors of kings and commoners, priests and princes, beggars and basketmakers."

And she set to work at once.

The third was an old, withered crone.

"I shall cut the threads of life," she sang as she opened a great pair of shears. "I shall snip the lives of all men and women, old and young, rich or poor. My scissors will cut every thread when the time is right."

And she set to work at once.

The three women came to be known to men and gods as the Fates. They sat together working at their great tapestry of life, and nothing and nobody could persuade them to change or move a single thread.

Although the gods gave them precious gifts and men and women prayed to them every day for the life of a child or a loved one, their power was so great that they just went on spinning and measuring and snipping without ever once taking any notice.

Their tapestry grew and grew and became more and more complicated as time went by. And it will go on growing till the world ends and Nyx's cloak covers the universe once more.

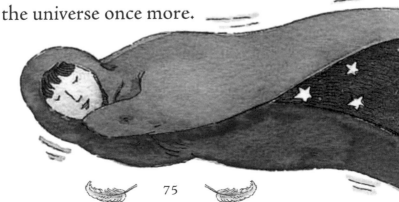

Greek Beasts and Heroes and where to find them...

Golden apples seem to cause a lot of trouble! Read more about Eris and her golden apple in "The Goddesses' Quarrel", which you'll find in *The Dragon's Teeth*. Brave Heracles had to get past a dragon and steal three golden apples for one of his twelve labours. But did he succeed? Look for "The Golden Apples" in *The Flying Horse* to find out. The story of "The Girl Who Ran Fastest" contains a sneaky trick with golden apples too. Turn to *The Harp of Death*.

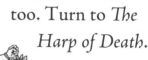

 76

Where did the Titans come from? Atticus's very first story will tell you. It's called "Father Sky and Mother Earth" and it's in *The Beasts in the Jar*. "The Three Gifts" is another story about the Titans which you'll find in the same book.

Crafty Hermes pops up all over the place in Atticus's stories. He's particularly useful to Perseus in his quest to kill "The Snake-Haired Gorgon". You can read all about it in *The Magic Head*.

Find out what happened when Sisyphus made the mistake of crossing Zeus in "The Sharp-Eyed King", a story in *The Dolphin's Message*. Bellerophon was the grandson of Sisyphus Sharp-Eyes, and he had only one dream in his life – to ride on the back of the great winged horse, Pegasus. His story is in *The Flying Horse*.

Orion's best friend and cousin was Artemis the huntress, and they used to hunt together. One of their adventures is told in "The Starry Hunter" which you'll find in *The Dolphin's Message*.

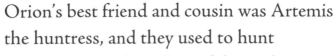

Boastful Arachne is almost as good at weaving as the Fates. Find out what happens when Athene challenges her to a weaving competition in "The Web Spinner" in *The Monster in the Maze*.

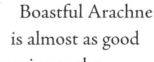

Greek Beasts and Heroes
have you read them all?